WordPress

A Comprehensive Beginners Guide For Creating Your Own Website Or Blog

© Copyright 2015

All rights reserved. No part of this book may be reproduced or transmitted in any form or by any means, electronically or mechanically, including photocopy, recording, or by any information storage or retrieval system, without the written permission from the publisher, except in the case of brief quotations embodied in critical articles or reviews.

Trademarks are the property of their respective holders. When used, trademarks are for the benefit of the trademark owner only.

DISCLAIMER

The information provided herein is stated to be truthful and consistent, in that any liability, in terms of inattention or otherwise, by any usage or abuse of any policies, processes, or directions contained within is the solitary and utter responsibility of the recipient reader. Under no circumstances will any legal responsibility or blame be held against the publisher for any reparation, damages, or monetary loss due to the information herein, either directly or indirectly. Respective authors hold all rights not held by publisher.

Book Description

This book, **WordPress:** *A Comprehensive Beginner's Guide For Creating Your Own Website Or Blog* is written for the person that wants to develop their own presence on the internet but don't know where to begin.

In this book we teach you the difference between WordPress.org and WordPress.com.
- How to build a WordPress powered website
- How to choose a host for your website
- The pros and cons of a free theme vs. a premium theme
- How to install a theme and how to test it for weightiness
- How to modify menus so that they say what you want
- How to install widgets and make a custom widget substitute for a menu
- How to write a blog post and make it readable by search engines and readers alike
- How to maintain readers, keeping their attention, posting consistently
- What is SEO and how to use it to your advantage
- The difference between a page and a post
- Internal links
- Permalinks
- Criticism
- Comments
- Do's and Don'ts of using WordPress

Although this isn't everything you ever wanted to know about WordPress, it is a good basic instruction guide for the person who has never dreamed of writing a blog or building their own webpage because they weren't technically inclined.

This book will get you through the initial process of setting up a WordPress theme, show you how to enhance the theme, and get you started blogging or selling your product.
Download this book now!

Table of Contents

Introduction
Chapter One: What Is WordPress?
    The Popularity of WordPress Themes
    Free Cost of WordPress Themes
    WordPress Codex, the Online Manual for WordPress Users
Chapter Two: What are the Difference Between WordPress.com and WordPress.org?
    Comparing WordPress.com to WordPress.org as Website Hosts
    The Basics of WordPress.com
    The Basics of WordPress.org
Chapter Three: Setting up WordPress
    5-minute install on Windows
    5-minute install on Mac
    Installing WordPress on Chrome
    Free Vs. Premium Themes
    Fast Loading Themes vs. Slow Loading Themes and How to Test
    What is a Responsive Theme?
    SEO Friendly Themes
    Vendors for Web Hosting Besides WordPress
Chapter Five: Starting a Website/Blog and Posting Content
    Page or Post?
    Hints for Blogging
    Making Your Pages more Interesting with Media
    Inserting an Image into a Blog Post
    Tagging Your Pages and Posts
Chapter Six: Designing Your Website Using Plugins
    How to Install a Plugin

      Free Plugins from WordPress
      The Top Ten Social Media Plugins
Chapter Seven: Creating and Customizing Menus
      To install a menu
      To link to a menu
      Adding your menu to your website
      To Reorder your Menu
      Suggestions for Uses of Menus
Chapter Eight: Installing Widgets
      Installing a Widget
      Creating a Custom Menu in the Widget Function
Chapter Nine: What is SEO and How Do I Use It?
      How SEO Ranks a Web Page
      No No's for SEO
      Basics for your website
      Optimize all social media venues
      Titles are very important with SEO
Chapter Ten: Using Yoast
      Features of Yoast SEO Plugin
      Robots Meta Configuration
      Breadcrumbs
      Permalink Simplifying
Chapter Eleven: Website/Blog Development, Drawing Traffic, Getting Readers, Maintaining Interest
      Website Development
      Decide What the Website is About
      What or Who is Your Target Market?
      Be Original
      The Importance of Honesty
      Handling Criticism and Praise
      Tips on the Comments Sections
      Five Tips to get People to Stay and Read
      Maintaining Interest with Consistent Posts
      Blog Techniques for Keeping Interest

>> Utilizing Your Subscription List
>> Begin with Adding a Contact Form Plugin
>> What to do with your Subscription List
> Chapter Twelve: Best Practices & Common Mistakes
>> Do's and Don'ts for WordPress Designed Websites
>> Do's
>> Don'ts
> Chapter Thirteen: Conclusion

Introduction

Thank you for downloading **WordPress: A Comprehensive Beginner's Guide For Creating Your Own Website Or Blog.**

In this book we teach you the basics of how to choose a web host, choose a WordPress template, install a WordPress template on your Mac, PC, or Chromebook, how to expand your theme to include menus, widgets, and plugins, and how to keep current with your WordPress theme.

We also discuss WordPress Free versus WordPress Premium themes and the responsibilities of owning either.

We discuss the basics of blogging, how to write a paragraph, and how to framework a post. We give instructions on how to insert media into a post, how to create tags, and keywords.

We detail information about SEO, links and search engine friendly web pages.

We conclude the book with the do's and don'ts to use and avoid when designing a web page.

Chapter One: What Is WordPress?

In this chapter, you will learn:

Key idea 1
WordPress is a free website building tool that is user friendly.

Key idea 2
WordPress Codex is the online manual for all WordPress functions and is also free on WordPress.org.

WordPress is a free website building tool that is supplies themes with plugins and menus for site customization. This is an open source CMS, content-management system, that is updated daily from contacts worldwide. The templates are written in PHP and MYSQL.

The Popularity of WordPress Themes

As of January, 2015, it was used by 23% of the top bloggers on the Web. WordPress currently has more than 60 million bloggers using its free themes.

WordPress themes are user friendly. You don't have to know code to build or update a WordPress website. You can add plugins and menus and widgets, all which will be explained in later chapters.

WordPress keywords are searched for more than 37 million times a month. Think of the traffic than can be routed to your website with the right keyword focus in your blog. How would your world change with just 1% of that number, or 37,000 hits a month? I would hope it would change drastically, and in a good way.

WordPress themes are translatable into 40 different languages. If English isn't your first language, or you just want to expand your reading audience or customer base, you can offer a website in another language like Croatian, or Spanish, or German. Just click the translate button and you have a new potential customer base.

WordPress is more popular than Amazon, with over 126 million visitors a month to their website, as opposed to Amazon's mere 96 million.

WordPress offers more than 29,000 free plugins for their customer use. No wonder I only list the top 10 in this book. I would be writing for months to list all 29,000. Thank goodness they are organized and indexed with a search box for you to find the one to suit your needs.

Free Cost of WordPress Themes

Did I mention WordPress themes are Free? There are thousands of WordPress themes you can use to build your website, and the majority of them are free. Those that are not free have tech support and offer, "I'll hold your hand management" for usually under $100 a year.

WordPress users have the luxury of switching themes as often as they like without having to rebuild the website, rewrite the blog entries, or uploading more pictures and illustrations. When you place a new theme an old theme the WordPress theme grafts the old information to the new site immediately with the press of a button.

WordPress Codex, the Online Manual for WordPress Users

WordPress Codex is available for those who want to venture into a more complicated version of WordPress. It is also free and on the website WordPress.org. WordPress.org gives support for the codex to all users. It has chapters on theme development, changing themes, WordPress lessons, and an update reference manual for all things related to WordPress development. It is being updated and improved around the clock, 24 hours a day.

There is a difference in being hosted by WordPress.com and other hosting organizations. WordPress.com has limitations on the websites that it hosts. Some of these limitations involve the number of ads that can be placed on the website. Other considerations are costs and domain names, maintenance and support issues.

Chapter Two: What is the Difference Between WordPress.com and WordPress.org?

In this chapter, you will learn:

Key idea 1
WordPress.com **is less expensive to utilize but has more constraints on the sitebuilder.**

Key idea 2
WordPress.org **costs more but has more autonomy and less restriction.**

The main difference between WordPress.com and WordPress.org is the host for your webpage. WordPress.com is a hosting platform that will give you a landing site, or webpage, for free. WordPress.org offers support for your website but you are the host. If they are your host provider they have different price points, all total less than $50 a month.

When you are the host, your purchase the lease for your page from a host site like GoDaddy, HostGator, or any number of servers. The cost is determined by the server. It can be anything from $1 to several hundred a month. The high-end fee providers offer to customize your website, build it for you, and maintain it.

WordPress.org is the site where the themes are offered. There are hundreds of free themes available. Before shopping for your theme, try to discern what you want your web page to look like. Do you want a lot of pictures? Do you want mostly text? Do want to be able to share with social media? Do you want conversations with your readers?

Are you going to have a newsletter, a regular posting schedule, or updates? Do you want RSS feed so that viewers can subscribe?

Comparing WordPress.com to WordPress.org as Website Hosts

A basic WordPress.com site can be free, but your domain name will be $18+ a year. It costs $30 a year for no ads on your site. It also costs for storage space, but 3GB a year is provided gratis.

A basic WordPress.org site is approximately $10 a year for your domain name, $5-$10 a month for hosting, unlimited storage space, and there are no ads.

The Basics of WordPress.com

A basic WordPress.com plan is free, as long as you don't mind WordPress ads, are content with no modifications to their free themes, and don't need a custom domain name.

The premium plan from WordPress.com offers a custom domain name, free mapping of the site, 13 GB of storage space, no advertisements from WordPress, custom videoPress, email for the site, and blog, all for $99 per year, including support from WordPress.

The business plan from WordPress.com includes everything in the premium plan, plus unlimited storage space, plus eCommerce, live chat support, unlimited premium themes per site and per blog, all for $299 a year.

Limitations with WordPress.com sites include no custom plugins, you can't run Google Adsense analytics on their sites, must use WordPress themes, and you have to pay to run ad-free from WordPress advertisements.

The Basics of WordPress.org

Using WordPress.org you will not have these limitations, but you will also be doing the maintenance on the site.

If you would rather not do any site maintenance, then WordPress.com is the better choice for you.

If you use WordPress.org, these will be your responsibilities in regards to site maintenance and development:

- Installing your wp site, includes set up
- Setting up your server
- Updating themes and plugins regularly as they are modified
- Updating your WordPress version
- Keeping your site secure from viruses and hackers
- Backing up your site regularly
- Resolving server problems.

Chapter Three: Setting up WordPress

In this chapter, you will learn:

Key idea 1
Choosing your theme is very subjective and based on your needs and taste.

Key idea 2
Picking the right theme for your installation will be trial and error. Once installed, you will be able to tweak to your specific needs.

WordPress is so easy to install that you mostly need to decide the criteria you need for your personal webpage.

5 minute install on Windows

1. You must have administrator rights on your machine
2. WordPress works for XP Professional, 7, 8, Vista and Server
3. If you already have Windows Platform Installer, it will prompt the next step
4. Install Windows PI if you haven't already
5. Configure the database according to the screen instructions, WordPress will evaluate what you need and give a prompt
6. If it asks for a password, enter one and write it down. It will ask for it again.
7. Choose your site to install wp on. Remember username and password.
8. Click Launch in the browser, WordPress will launch.

If you have any issues at all, consult the codes at WordPress.org.

5 minute install on Mac

1. You must have MAMP installed. MAMP can be found at the MAMP website.

2. Click on Preferences. Then click Ports, which will default to Apache.
3. Click Start Servers.
4. Download WordPress.
5. Click and drag all of the files in WordPress to your MAMP folder.
6. Go to your local site and enter this:
   ```
   Database Name: WordPress
   Username (database): root
   Password (database): root
   Database Host/server: localhost
   Table Prefix: wp_
   ```
7. Make a memo that the name of the database is WordPress. Make sure this is what you entered for your database name. If it isn't, change it to match.
8. Enter your blog name and email address. You should be set up.

Installing WordPress on Chrome

1. Go to the Chrome Apps store.
2. Find the WordPress app.
3. Install.
4. This will take you to the WordPress tutorial.
5. Follow the steps, enter the domain name.
6. If you are not using WordPress.com as your host
7. Browse the thousands of free themes until you choose a few to download.

Now choose a theme from WordPress.org/themes.

Download your theme onto your computer. This will be a zipped file.

Go to your WordPress site. Enter the Admin panel with your username and password.

Go to themes. Enter the control panel. Select theme. Select new theme. Upload new theme. Select Activate theme. Select "custom".

Now you are in the theme's customizer file.

Select your colors, logo, menus, and widgets from those offered by the theme.

If you don't see what you like, read carefully the parameters of the theme.

Those choices may not be available for the theme you've chosen. Go with the flow and pick the one you like best. If color is especially important to you, go back and choose a theme that says in the description, customizable colors and fonts.

For the free themes, some themes only allow specific colors, or specific sizes of pictures, or specific widgets or menus. You can always add menus by customizing the widgets or menus. This will be discussed in a later chapter. If you cannot download a specific theme, or WordPress says the theme is broken, pick another theme. Some operating systems are not compatible with some WordPress themes. It is a trial and error method of finding the right theme that works for you, your machine, and your host.

Free Vs. Premium Themes

hen one thinks of free, usually the first phrase that comes to mind is, "you get what you pay for". This was unfortunately a true statement even in the case of WordPress in the past. Things have changed now, and there are more than 1,600 free themes with which to build your web page. Below I have outlined the pros and cons of a free theme versus a premium theme.

The Pros
- Premium themes are updated frequently, meaning that the bad links and odd or broken codes are quickly repaired for a smoother experience for yourself and your readers. This is very important as a badly maintained theme can lose your customers and readers.
- Premium themes are more unique. Free themes, because of their price, can be seen coming and going on the Internet. There will be likely thousands of people using the same theme and framework as your website.
- The premium themes have better documentation, which enables them to have a better performance. Premium themes often offer a PDF file explaining the options and preferred widgets and plugins for modifications. They have expanded capabilities and customizable fonts and colors. These are rarely offered on a free theme.
- When you purchase a premium theme, you are offered website support. This support is continued as long as you are subscribed to the theme. There may be a live chat available, email, and a customer forum for troubleshooting issues. Free themes may have a forum, but that will be the extent of the support.

- There are no links required for an advertisement. Often free themes require an attribution link at the bottom of the webpage.

The Cons
- Cost. Free themes are free. Premium themes start at $39 and go into the hundreds. If you are a start up business, money will be tight and this is somewhere you can skimp.
- The Premium themes have more complicated configurations. This may be beyond your abilities and you might have to hire someone to install your theme. This increases the price of the theme.
- You may be paying for more than you want or need. Most customers surveyed were not happy with pages that had sliders or extra bells and whistles. This was more for the Webmaster to maintain and was confusing for the customer. Too many choices for a consumer can lead to a quick abandonment of a webpage.
- The customization screen can be very confusing for the installer. Each theme has the same categories, but sometimes the categories are used differently. In loading themes, I have noticed several have no obvious way to add a photo on the front page, even though that is touted as a selling point. The more customization options will add more confusing terms and properties you might not even desire.
- The best way to evaluate a theme is to log onto the public forum. Read the issues mentioned. I have a Chromebook for my fast internet use and many themes

crash the Chromebook. It is very important to make sure you are not downloading a broken theme, as your response will be frustration. In addition, you will lose time and even copy if the theme is broken.

Fast Loading Themes vs. Slow Loading Themes and How to Test

A very important issue for a web theme is the loading time. Themes that are heavy with sliders and extra widgets will take longer to load. The longer load time is a disadvantage to the search engines and will result in a lower ranking for your page. What kinds of things will slow the loading time?
- Feature heavy themes
- Lots of sliders, more than 3
- Pre-installed widgets, more than 5
- Extra JavaScript using animation
- Bigger files
- Poor coding, check the customer forum for complaints
- Poorly maintained or rarely updated, check the update history

To test your theme, go to Pingdom Website Speed Test, enter your theme URL from the demo, and check for the HTTP requests. The requests should be less than 20, the time should take less than 1 second, and the bandwidth should be minimal, less than 20. If your numbers are larger than this, you will have issues with lag and lower rankings.

There are several sites that sell themes. I am not recommending a particular site, as I don't want to fill this book with promotional material. Just Google Premium WordPress Themes and the vendors will jump at the chance to sell you their product.

What is a Responsive Theme?

A responsive theme is one that is friendly to mobile devices. Since more than 40% of Internet traffic is now from tablets and smartphones, it is important to install a responsive theme on your website. Immediately eliminate any theme that does not say responsive in the theme description of attributes. You do not want to omit 40% of your customer base or readers.

After you have picked your theme, test the demo on Google's mobile-friendliness tool. Enter the demo version of the theme and see how it responds to your mobile device.

SEO Friendly Themes

Look for themes that say SEO friendly or SEO optimized. Specific things that you need for options on your website are header tags and alt tags. You also want Meta descriptions, keywords, and short urls.

Chapter Four: Choosing Your Hosting Provider

In this chapter, you will learn:

Key idea 1
Pick your host according to your needs. Examine your contract carefully.

Key idea 2
If you have little need for business services, go with the free WordPress.com web hosting.

When searching for a web host provider, determine your needs before looking at price points. Web host providers offer differing services for selective price packages. Some offer email, some offer shared serving, some offer limited or no support, and some offer private hosting with all the bells and whistles for an extensive hosting package. If you are a start up business, you might want to keep a low cost server for the first year.

If you are looking for a site builder included in your hosting plan, read the small print of the contract and make sure you have access to a site builder. Some hosts do only that, host with a specific amount of storage space. Make sure you know what you are paying for. Other tools that are available are email marketing tools and shopping cart applications. Know what you need before you sign a contract.

Spam and malware are issues when hosting a website. See if your host offers security protection specific tools and if they offer a good service plan.

If you are just wanting to blog and show a few family photos, then go with the free WordPress.com website and service. If you have need of just a little more, go with the WordPress.org website service. These are designed for the beginning website and blogger that just wants a presence on the Internet, but not a full-blown store with all the bells and whistles.

On the other hand, if you are a brick and mortar business that has a strong presence in the street and wants the same presence on the internet, expect to invest some money to get a premium website that will allow shopping, give you email contacts, and send daily notes to your customers about specials and sales.

Vendors for Web Hosting Besides WordPress

Siteground web hosting at approximately $10 a month will give good business support for small businesses, has a solid reputation for security, and has easy to learn tutorials regarding extra features and business opportunities.

GoDaddy for $4 has a good product that meshes well with Microsoft email products.

Liquid Web hosting at $15 a month has a good product and VPS and dedicated hosting plans. You pay more with Liquid Web, but for a larger business you get the needed support and safety net.

InMotion Shared is $4 and offers the most services for the least price for a small business owner or individual expecting a lot of traffic.

Chapter Five: Starting a Website/Blog and Posting Content

In this chapter, you will learn:

Key idea 1
Starting a website allows you to have a personal window to the world.

Key idea 2
Your blog is your opportunity to have a dialogue with new people.

Now you are at the fun part. You have picked a host. You have set up your site. You have installed a theme and designed the web page just as you like.

Now you get to talk, well, blog. You want content that is interesting to your readers. What are your hobbies? Is this a personal blog? You will need to set up pages and posts.

Page or Post?

Pages are permanents, static places that are on your website for information. Examples of static pages are About, Home, Content, Start Here, Books, Events, Archives, Recent Awards, etc. These are the reference materials for your readers. Pages are also where you would offer an enrollment form for email, a newsletter, or an event.

In contrast, posts are transient, current event articles. Posts are your reflections of the day, your comments on news events, your political statements, etc. Posts should be changed often to keep interest high, but pages and their information are semi-permanent. Be sure and create internal links from posts to pages and vice versa.

Hints for Blogging

Begin by placing a picture of yourself prominently on your blog. People relate to photos much better than typeset, even when they resonate with your ideas and passion. People just want to see a familiar face with whom they can relate and respond.

When starting a blog, the blank page may just frighten you a little. It does most writers. Remember there were very good reasons you started the blog. Hopefully you wrote them down, but here are our best thoughts on the subject.

- You had something you wanted to say to the world on a regular basis
- You wanted to improve your writing skills
- You wanted a more intentional life, one with reflection, maybe a journal of sorts
- You wanted to design who you are, and refine your thoughts and dreams
- You want to develop a disciplined life, for the heart and health benefits
- You wanted discernment in your life. By necessity, as you have to focus when blogging, discernment becomes a second nature to you.

- You want to meet new people. Just allowing comments on your blog will bring you in contact with new people and new ideas.
- You'll be more comfortable within yourself. At first you feel very vulnerable allowing your thoughts to escape the privacy of your mind and venture into the world of criticism and public opinion. Later, though, you begin to own those thoughts in an assertive manner and learn to make your voice heard.
- You'll begin to understand the world better, and other people. It will make you a more compassionate person.
- You want to help change the world with your ideas and opinions.

Making Your Pages more Interesting with Media

When staring at a white surface with paragraphs of copy, some people get very bored very easily. You have just 12 seconds to attract the attention of the reader. You have a total of 96 seconds for their full attention span in an entire day.

The best way to attract attention is with the addition of media. Inserting images into your blog post gives the reader a place to frame their attention, and may incite their curiosity. Pick a representative image of your blog post or page main idea, and place it into the blog.

Inserting an Image into a Blog Post

1. Find your image in your photographs or on the Internet with a free image site like Pixabay.

2. Make sure this image is available for distribution or pay the rights to publish it.
3. Download the image to your hard drive.
4. Go to your theme administration page.
5. Click Media
6. Click upload file
7. Click the file to load
8. Watch the file upload
9. Click this file
10. Click add to post
11. Position the file in the post on the right, left or center
12. You have now added an image
13. Save your post
14. Go to the top left under your name and click visit site
15. Look at your page carefully. You may see errors.
16. If you do, hit edit post. Fix the errors. Update.

Tagging Your Pages and Posts

Tags are used by search engines to categorize your posts for potential readers. Over in the right hand column you will see a place to enter tags. What you want to enter is your keyword term and other descriptive tags. If you are, for example, advertising a product like free eBooks, then your tag should be "free eBooks," and "free download books," then maybe the subject of the book, "free Arthritis Relief book". As the search engine reads the tag, it creates a web link to all posts that utilize the same tag.

Since your tag will be lumped in with thousands of other like tags, you want your title of your blog page to be both informative and clever. Your title should list your tag word and your product name, or brand name. The URL for your page should also include the tag word, in addition to the brand.

Chapter Six: Designing Your Website Using Plugins

In this chapter, you will learn:

**Key idea 1
Plugins allow you to enhance and expand your functions on your website.**

**Key idea 2
There are hundreds of free plugins on <u>WordPress</u>.**

Plugins are bits and pieces of software offered by WordPress to enhance and extend the functions on your site. <u>WordPress plugins link here</u>.

How to Install a Plugin

You can install plugins from your admin area in your WordPress theme. Download the plugin onto your computer. Log into WordPress admin. Click on Plugins, then Add New. Browse to the plugin desired and select. Click Install Now. Click Activate. You've now installed the plugin.

Free Plugins from WordPress

There are literally thousands of free plugins from WordPress; here are a few of the most popular and their functions:

<u>Contact Form 7</u> - a generic contact form you can place on your site for friends or customers wishing contact from you.

Wordfence Security - protects your website from hackers and malware for free.

Google Analytics by Yoast - allows you to see the traffic you receive on your website

Akismet - guards against spam comments.

Breadcrumb NavXT - shows visitors, where they came from and where they are going

TablePress - for embedding tables into your posts without writing code

bbPress - forum software for hosting a bulletin board forum

All-in-one WordPress Security and Firewall - by WordPress, offers both security for your site and a firewall for protection, very user friendly

Jetpack by WordPress - moves everything more quickly, gives visitor stats. Crashes my Chromebook but you may not have an issue.

BuddyPress - helps you run a social network with profiles for users, have private chats, etc. It is an excellent resource for a sports team or running club to have a private place to meet.

Really Simple CAPTCHA - use this with forms as a way to weed out robots.

The Top Ten Social Media Plugins

Social media is so important to continue to build your web page presence. Don't you want your readers to be able to share your content on Facebook, Twitter, Reddit, or Google Plus? Any one of these 10 plugins can do the job well.

1. Digg Digg, has the options of both like and share for Facebook
2. Flare has the option of a Follow Me widget that builds your subscription list
3. ShareThis has a floating bar with the social media buttons that follows the reader on the page or post
4. Share Buttons by AddThis gives you free analytics when the share button is used
5. Floating Social Media Icon has a bar that jumps onto the screen for the reader to share your posts
6. Social Media Feather supports shortcodes for the iPhone and iPad.
7. Slick Social Sharing Buttons allows you to place specific social media icons on specific posts and pages, also allows customizable buttons
8. Social Media Widget is one of the easiest products to use, and has animated buttons
9. Shareaholic allows your posts to be shared to other social media sites while gathering analytics for you like how many shares and where they go
10. AddToAny Sharebuttons shares to over 100 social media sites and in more than a dozen languages.

Chapter Seven: Creating and Customizing Menus

In this chapter, you will learn:

Key idea 1
Menus allow easy navigation through the website.

Key idea 2
Custom menus allow you to link pages, posts, or outside links to your page.

Menus in your WordPress themes allow you to navigate through your pages by links, posts, pages or any other tools. Menus can be customized to have specialized links to outside content and interior content, both.

For example, if you wish to sell a book on your site, you can list the titles in your menu of Current Books for Sale, and then link the title specifically to the Amazon page where it is sold. If you are entering a competition, you can link outward to the competition page, and link inward to a signup page for your booster club or other competitors.

Other custom menu suggestions are a list of current events or book signings for your offerings.

To install a menu
You first must define the menu in your WordPress theme.
1. Go to your WordPress dashboard
2. Click on Appearance
3. Click Menus
4. Click Create New Menu
5. Name your Menu
6. Save your menu.

To link to a menu
1. Go to the Pages section
2. Click View All, this will show you the current pages on your website
3. Click each box next to the pages you want on the menu

4. Click Add to Menu
5. Click Save Menu

Adding your menu to your website

1. Go to Theme locations in the menu window
2. Click the box where you want your menu to appear. There may be several choices, depending on your theme.
3. Click Save Menu.

To Reorder your Menu

1. Click the pencil icon on the menu screen
2. Click the Move button
3. Click Move the menu up or down
4. Click Save

Suggestions for Uses of Menus

- Menus of Pages
- Menus of Posts
- Menus to Link to Outside Sites, like links to purchase products
- Menus for Categories, for example all posts about grandchildren
- Menus for Specific Tags, for example all posts with the tag free items

If your theme does not have enough menus, you can add one as a widget.

Chapter Eight: Installing Widgets

In this chapter, you will learn:

Key idea 1
Widgets list information on your page like post names, pages, etc.

Key idea 2
You can customize a widget to add a menu where there is none.

Widgets are small blocks of text on your website that perform specific functions that you can customize. Examples of widgets are posts and pages listings, a calendar of recent posts, a list of contact information, a custom contact form, or an email address.

Widgets are easy to manage and require no coding experience. To install a widget, you just click and drag it to the widget area on the setup page.

Installing a Widget

Go to the WordPress administration area. Click on Appearance, then Widgets. You will be given a list of the widgets that are included with your theme, plus any extra widgets you have installed for convenience.

Click on the widget on the left side of the screen and drag it to the right side under the place you wish it to appear.

If you need help with your widgets, click the help icon at the top of the screen on your WordPress widget page. There will be detailed instructions for assistance with your widgets.

Creating a Custom Menu in the Widget Function

1. Install the plugin titled [Custom Menu Wizard Widget](#).
2. On the Widget page, drag the custom menu to the right sidebars
3. Select the menus you want to display
4. Save the widget.
5. It's that easy!

Chapter Nine: What is SEO and How Do I Use It?

In this chapter, you will learn:

Key idea 1
SEO stands for Search Engine Optimization, the utility that ranks websites on the Internet.

Key idea 2
The higher your page is ranked by SEO, the more visitors you will attract.

SEO is Search Engine Optimization, a method of attracting visitors and readers to your website by earning high rankings on Google, Bing, and Yahoo, for example. Google, Bing, and Yahoo are Search Engine Results Pages, SERPs, that categorize your rankings of the website by your content, performance, authority, and user experience.

How SEO Ranks a Web Page

- Content is valued by the theme, the text, the titles and descriptions on the page.
- Performance is measured by how fast your site runs and does it work
- Authority is the depth of your content. Are other people linking your content like you are a reference page? This makes a higher ranking in the SERPs.
- User experience is the look and eye appeal of your site. It is easy to navigate? Do you have a high bounce rate, i.e. do people visit your page and immediately leave? Can you hold the interest of the reader?

No No's for SEO

- Stuffing Keywords, search engines don't like it if you over utilize your keywords
- Paid Links, search engines aren't impressed by paid links
- Too Hard to Navigate, if your website has poor navigation, very few menus, an overabundance of ads, or too much clutter, the search engine will downgrade your ranking.

Basics for your website

- Do you know why you have a website?
- What is the goal of your website?
- How do you know it is successful?
- It is motivated by sales? Or readers?

Optimize all social media venues

- Facebook
- Twitter
- LinkedIn
- Google Plus
- Email
- Instagram

Make sure you have a presence on each of these sites, and radio and television.

WordPress offers a free [SEO plugin](#) that makes your website more search engine friendly. Be sure to download it and activate it.

Titles are very important with SEO

Keep in mind these tips when titling a blog post.
- Your Focus keyword should be at the beginning of your title. This is for the search engine to locate.
- Your brand should be at the end of your title, again for the search engine.
- The rest of the title should be catchy, to attract attention from the readers.

Meta keywords are no longer searched by search engines so ignore them. Meta descriptions are read by real people, so make the characters count. Start your Meta description with your focus keyword, and then make as interesting a synopsis of your blog post as you can. Try to pull the reader into your story by the teaser of reading the Meta description.

Breadcrumbs should be added to your website to help the reader navigate the website. Breadcrumbs should be on the single pages and on the single posts. The breadcrumbs should link a reader back to the home page.

Entice your readers to subscribe to your website and blog. Offer more than one subscription point for the reader. An RSS subscribe button is a very important resource for you to install. Using a weekly email subscription service, like Mailchimp, can be invaluable for keeping up with contacts.

Chapter Ten: Using Yoast

In this chapter, you will learn:

Key idea 1
Yoast SEO plugin by WordPress has complete features to track traffic coming and going from your website.

Key idea 2
Knowing the source of your traffic lets you focus on how to increase your customer base.

Yoast SEO plugin by WordPress is the most complete plugin for SEO customers. It has everything the client would want to analyze the traffic to their website. You have a snippet preview, page analysis, Meta descriptions, image titles, sitemaps and more optimization opportunities.

Features of Yoast SEO Plugin

- Yoast SEO lets you title your own features
- Write your own meta descriptions
- Use a pre-written template
- Has a snippet preview to see what shows in Google
- Offers a focus keyword for search engines

Robots Meta Configuration

Sometimes we write posts or pages that we don't want the whole world to see. Yoast SEO has an advanced feature that allows you to hide pages or posts on a single post basis. This means that you can keep the wholesale price list available for employees but hide it from the general public on your website.

Breadcrumbs

Yoast SEO offers breadcrumbs that bring your customer or reader back to the home page when they are lost on your page. You can control what the post says and the path it follows home, instead of a pre-programmed response.

Permalink Simplifying

Yoast makes permalinks work like a dream. It cleans up the extra stuff people put at the end of links that garbled the instructions to the user. No more weird /2 links or extra characters, numbers and symbols. Simplifying the permalinks ensures smooth sailing for the search engines to navigate their way to your website.

Chapter Eleven: Website/Blog Development, Drawing Traffic, Getting Readers, Maintaining Interest

In this chapter, you will learn:

Key idea 1
Website development is the coding and maintenance of a website.

Key idea 2
WordPress takes the work out of website development so that you can focus on the creative side, the look and feel of your website.

Website Development

Website development is normally about coding and updates and the technical side of the website. WordPress took all that out of the picture when it introduce the theme concept. Now website development is about drawing traffic, writing skills, getting readers and keeping the readers coming back to your blog.

Decide What the Website is About

Now we tap into the creative side of you. This is the part that is all about you, your passion and your place in the world. What do you want to say? Are you opposed to smoking? Are you for recycling? Have you decided to downsize and used to living in the upsize?

Find your spot, your niche, and your passion. What do you love to talk about all day long?

This is your place to indulge in all the conversation you want to share.

What or Who is Your Target Market?

Who are your readers? Who is your target market? Do you want to speak to like-minded individuals, or are you really wanting a discourse with more than one opinion?

If you are writing about your family and its trials and tribulations, your target market would be other family members and friends. If you are writing about restoring old boats or building one in your basement like Gibbs on NCIS, then your target market will be other restorers and the few curious souls like myself who want to know how you get the boat out of the basement.

Target your content to your readers. Identify whom they are and what they want to hear. The only way to attract consistent quality readers is to add value and meaning to their lives. If you don't give them substance, they won't come back.

Be Original

Give original content. Don't copy a news headline from the Internet and say, isn't this sad? People see this hundreds of times a day on their Facebook feed. Give them something to chew on, which is your unique perspective. What makes your blog different from the million or so out there? You. You are the uniqueness of this blog. Create. Show people who you are and what you believe.

Be interesting and original. Is your quirkiness part of your boat building? Do you have to finish the sail before you start the stern? What is your special part? This is what others want to hear, why you are different and how. Engage your reader by discussing the details of boat building, or book selling, or even family reunions.

The Importance of Honesty

Be honest with yourself and others. If you are having a ho-hum day, say so. Don't drone on and on about the bad things in life, but be honest if they are dragging you down. Not everybody has up days all the time. You want people to feel like you are a real person, not a robot, and not Mr. Chirpy.

Spend more time writing than designing your site. You can get caught up in tweaking the themes and forget about the writing. (Ask me how I know.) Don't drop the purpose for the window dressing. A really good-looking site is nice, but not if the content is drivel.

Find your voice and define your purpose. If need be, write a mission statement so that you know who you are and what you are about. Use Social Media to expand your audience but don't get so wrapped up in Social Media that you forget and neglect your blog.

Research what you're writing about so you sound relevant, not ignorant. Don't make blanket statements instead research the facts. Express your informed opinion in a clear and succinct post. Don't rant.

Remove everything from your blog that takes away from your message. Just because you can install 100 widgets doesn't mean you need this distraction.

Handling Criticism and Praise

Ignore criticism. There will always be someone who doesn't like what you are doing or thinks they can manage or direct it better than you. Suggest they make their own blog.

How to handle criticism and praise with tact and grace. Examine each remark for truth. Hide the truth in your heart and bring it out to ponder for character improvement. Throw the criticism away. Enjoy the praise while you have it as it never lasts.

Tips on the Comments Sections

Make your comments section easy to use. Do not make the reader wait for approval or management before they can see their comments. You will have a few trolls who trash your comment section, but more importantly, you will have honest feedback from readers and customers. The number one detriment to having a rich comment section is the client's' necessity of approved clearance.

People want instant gratification. They want to see their comments quickly, not three days later and certainly not modified, no matter how ugly it gets.

Five Tips to get People to Stay and Read

1. Limit your post length to no less than 300 words and no more than 800 words. Break your content into short sentences and short paragraphs. Use visuals like numbering and bullet points.

2. Use a large font so your post can be read from a phone screen. One third of blog readers are doing so from their telephone or tablet. Make your font a 14 or 16 point font. You are currently reading a 12-point font. Our subtitles are 14 point. See the difference in the ease of reading? Make sure you are using solid black type instead of a pale grey, also. Use good contrast on your web page. Make your sentences no more than 75 characters long.
3. Write only about one thing at a time. Your blog post should be structured around one topic. If you have something to say about a different topic, start another post or page. What do you want to say to your readers? Be specific, stay on topic, and stay focused. You should be able to summarize your entire blog post in one sentence. If you can't, you need a good and honest editor.
4. Remember the rules of paragraph construction. Write your first sentence as your topic sentence. Your second sentence should modify or explain the first sentence. The third sentence should give more clarification to sentence 1. The fourth sentence should be the last explanation or addition, and the fifth and final sentence should conclude the paragraph by being a summary of sentence one.
5. Ensure your post is scannable by having headings and subheadings. Make sure you use topic sentences throughout the blog post. Keep on track with your writing by keeping it sharp. Edit for extra unnecessary words. Don't use the keywords more than three times in a post. Use it in the first sentence, somewhere in the middle of the post, and in the concluding sentence.

Maintaining Interest with Consistent Posts

- Have a plan before you write your first post. What do you want to say today to your customers or readers? What will be your call to action? Write down the framework of your blog post before you write the first blog post.
- Start writing with a clear structure. Introduce your topic, note what you will address in the body of the post, and write a conclusion to your post. Now write a one-sentence summary of the post. This is your framework of your post.
- Write in complete paragraphs. Use topic sentences. Use modifying sentences. Use concluding sentences that summarize the paragraph. Start a new paragraph with a new idea. Support the new idea with modifying sentences. Conclude the paragraph with a summary statement.
- Use Headings abundantly. They help the mind and the eye focus and search engines love them. Use subheadings to break down the information for the reader. Use keywords in your headings, but not every heading.
- Use words that signal your direction to the reader. Use words like first, second, and finally. Readers know this means there are three points, and after finally you will close the idea. Always proofread and spell check the article. Use a grammar checker also.
- Make the length of your article no less than 300 words and no more than 700 words. Use your keyword three times in the body of the article.
- Link your article back to previous content whenever you can make it work. This helps readers to read your previous posts and pages. Internal links move your rankings higher on Google.

- Regularly update your content so your readers expect to hear from you. This shows your reader, your customer and Google that you are still living and breathing.
- Offer a newsletter or a weekly post for your subscribers, something that is different than just popping by to read. You want consistent traffic to your website so offer the subscribers something special.
- Sponsor a giveaway to readers of your posts. It doesn't have to be expensive, but a giveaway attracts new readers and customers. You want to develop interest in your product, even if your product is you.

Blog Techniques for Keeping Interest

The following are blog techniques that are proven to keep the interest of readers. Utilize them when you feel you are becoming boring. If your posts are dry to you, I guarantee your readers are losing interest.

1. Make lists. Think about how popular David Letterman's lists are. You can become the next David Letterman of the Internet with your own Top 10 Lists.
2. Info-graphics. People like varied pieces of information in easily digestible bites. Offer time lines, charts, tables, and snippets of trivia on your website.
3. Tutorials. Everybody wants to learn something, and most want to learn it the easiest way possible. Give visual tutorials on how to...anything, for example show how to change the oil in the car, make a quilt, or self-publish a book. Creating informational content on a regular basis keeps people coming back to see what they will learn in the new lesson of the day, or week.
4. Offer Guide books as a resource for your readers or customers. Write a blog in stages about any topic that is

thoroughly researched. Offer the entire guide as an eBook. CreateSpace will publish the eBook for free, and now you have a series or guide to attract readers, and a freebie to offer as a prize for your subscribers. You can also offer the guide for sale on your web page.

5. Do some live blogging at a resort, concert, or political event. Record your impressions live, film a small video, and post the content immediately. Readers love to get the inside knowledge right when things are happening. Make your readers feel like they are with you in the concert hall.

6. News Round Ups are a popular way to give a synopsis of the day's happenings in the world of your special topic. If your topic is wrenches, write about the newest wrench developed by Craftsman, or their guarantee and how you've tested it, or the latest product promotion in the news round up. You can always pick up snippets of Headline News or Weird News of the Day to be shared with your readers.

7. Public Q&A sessions are people attracters, as people want to be heard. Offer a live Q&A session with you as the developer of a product, or an author, or maybe a mechanic. Knowing you are available as an instrument of reference will attract people to your useful store of knowledge.

8. Predictions and Projections on any topic from Nuclear Warheads to the Next Big Thing on the Internet. Talk about your views on the newest Apple product, or why you think Chromebooks will fail. Take a big leap and publish where you are on any issue. You will draw traffic, both good and bad. You will increase your readers and you may even go viral!

9. Interviews with personalities that are well known. Everybody is separated by another person by only six

degrees of separation. You know somebody who is related to someone else who is famous for something. Think a minute about your contacts. You may even have gone to high school with a publisher or an author or a successful songwriter. Your best friend's mother may be an artist with work in the Museum of Modern Art in New York City. Take a deep breath and call the connection for an interview. Do an email or phone interview and ask their permission to publish it on your blog. Their fans can be your fans with a good interview and a marketing plan for follow-up.

Utilizing Your Subscription List

When writing a blog, offer more than one contact point for subscribing to a daily update. Make one contact point a sign up form when they enter the blog. Make another contact opportunity with a pop up subscription form they have to close to read the page or post.

Begin with Adding a Contact Form Plugin

1. Go to WordPress and pick the plugin POWr Form Builder
2. Download to your computer, install on your theme page in the plugin section, and activate the POWr Form Builder
3. Place in widget, menu, footer, or place code in posts for a pop up
    - Free Features of POWr Form Builder
        - ☐ Custom fonts and colors to create your form for submission
        - ☐ Custom fields for text, dates, email, name

- ☐ Adds recurring payments to PayPal
- ☐ Custom Thank You messages for your clients
- ☐ Responsive for mobile devices
- ☐ Translateable for languages other than English
- ☐ You design the sign up form, not generic

What to do with your Subscription List

People like the personal touch of email. They can read the email with relative privacy, whereas reading a Facebook post or a twitter comment is a shared experience. Even reading your blog is much less personal than reading a targeted email.

Use the email subscription list sparingly. You don't want to bombard your email list with unnecessary and irrelevant information that they will think of as spam. Be sure that your emails are to the point and informative.

There is a 60% chance your email reader will click the link to your blog and continue reading your content, just because you sent them a personal email for their consideration. Send them news. Send them a discount coupon. Send them a giveaway chance. Announce your newest product or your newest child. Make your readers and customers In the Know first.

Chapter Twelve: Best Practices & Common Mistakes

Do's and Don'ts for WordPress Designed Websites

Do's

Pick an uncluttered theme that best represents what you want to say.

Fill your website with information, not clutter. When people see a cluttered website they think you are disorganized and sloppy. They become anxious that you can handle their ideas or their money appropriately because of this misconstrual of your skills.

Learn how to upgrade and manage your website for the satisfaction of learning a new skill.

You can hire someone to build and manage your website but it only takes practice and courage to do it yourself. Expand your skills and learn how to do everything for yourself. You will feel better for venturing out and your website will be a true reflection of you.

Get familiar with the WordPress Codex. It is not necessary to consult the online instruction manual but you need to know it is there.

There may be a day that the simple website isn't enough for your intellectual curiosity. This is the day you will open the

Codex and start learning new things about WordPress. When this day comes, don't get disgusted with yourself you didn't go there sooner.

Embrace the opportunity to learn and grow. Explore topics about plugins, menus, and widgets. Take the tutorials. Venture into video making.

Don'ts

Don't-Put so many widgets on your website that you slow down the processing. It may look cool on the back side of the web but it will slow the loading of your pages, which in turn, makes your readers frustrated and likely to abandon you.

You only have 12 seconds to attract their attention and 96 seconds of their entire day. Make the most of it by putting your webpage directly in front of them instantly.

Don't-Keep installing a widget, menu, plugin, or theme that crashes your system. Some of the newest themes don't have all the bugs worked out.

While searching for the perfect theme for my personal website, I went through at least 40 different themes. Probably 10 of them crashed my system. Another 3 plugins would not work on my system. I had one menu that would get lost in space. If it doesn't work, don't force it. Look for a similar product and go with it.

Don't-let the blogging or maintenance of your website become a chore. Make an organized effort to work and play on your website every day.

Try to find the unusual joy in life, not the mundane.

Make your blog express your inner insights on life, beauty, and the uncommon inspiration. Find a way to give back to the world. If you are a business, offer some type of contribution to the community. Pay them back for supporting you.

Chapter Thirteen: Conclusion

This book has been written to make it easy for you to install WordPress to your website. We have directed you in how to choose a host for your web page, be it WordPress.com, WordPress.org, or another commercial venture.

We have written instructions on how to install the WordPress theme on your Mac, PC, or a Chromebook. We have suggested the differences between a free WordPress theme and a Premium WordPress theme.

We have listed instructions on how to install and utilize plugins, widgets, and menus. We have discussed theme customizations and modifications.

SEO is an important tool to increase your traffic to your website and your readers. We recommend the Yoast SEO plugin to help you attract search engines and readers both.

Included in this book have been instructions on inserting media into posts and pages, the best length for a post, and the unwritten structure of a post. We have outlined how to write a paragraph and how to find the main theme of your post or page.

We have suggested ways to maintain your audience interest, how to set up a mailing list, how to offer a contact point, and what to do with comments and criticism of your blog, ideas, or product.

Finally, we have suggested ways to maintain your web page and your vibrancy. Enjoy your blog. Create your voice in the world. Make a contribution to yourself and your community.

Thank you again for downloading this book **WordPress: *Comprehensive Beginner's Guide For Creating Your Own Website Or Blog.***

I hope this book was able to help you to learn all the methods you need to create and install a WordPress website on your computer.

The next step is to begin blogging, photographing, and creating interesting content.

Finally, if you enjoyed this book, please take the time to share your thoughts and post a review on Amazon. It'd be greatly appreciated!

Thank you and good luck!

Printed in Great Britain
by Amazon